How a Book is Made

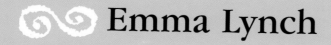 Emma Lynch

Heinemann Educational Publishers
Halley Court, Jordan Hill, Oxford OX2 8EJ
a division of Reed Educational & Professional Publishing Limited
www.heinemann.co.uk

Heinemann is a registered trademark of Reed Educational & Professional Publishing Limited

First published 2000
Original edition © Reed Educational & Professional Publishing Limited 1998
Literacy World Satellites edition © Reed Educational & Professional Publishing Limited 2000
Additional writing for Satellites edition by Wendy Cobb

04 03 02 01 00
10 9 8 7 6 5 4 3 2 1

ISBN 0 435 11894 3   *LW Satellites: How a Book is Made* single copy

ISBN 0 435 11898 6   *LW Satellites: How a Book is Made* 6 copy pack

Designed by Oxprint Design
Printed and bound in the UK

Acknowledgements
All photographs by Trevor Clifford

Also available at Stage 1 of *Literacy World Satellites*

ISBN 0 435 11893 5   *LW Satellites: Incredible Insects* single copy
ISBN 0 435 11897 8   *LW Satellites: Incredible Insects* 6 copy pack

ISBN 0 435 11891 9   *LW Satellites: The Search for Tutankhamen* single copy
ISBN 0 435 11895 1   *LW Satellites: The Search for Tutankhamen* 6 copy pack

ISBN 0 435 11892 7   *LW Satellites: Making the Past into Presents* single copy
ISBN 0 435 11896 X   *LW Satellites: Making the Past into Presents* 6 copy pack

ISBN 0 435 11900 1   *LW Satellites: Teacher's Guide Stage 1*
ISBN 0 435 11899 4   *LW Satellites: Guided Reading Cards Stage 1*

Contents

Halley Court
Jordan Hill
Oxford OX2 8EJ UK

Telephone +44 (0)1865 311366
Fax +44 (0)1865 314140
URL http://www.heinemann.co.uk
e-mail reed.educational@bhein.rel.co.uk
Direct Line

31 August 1998

Dear Reader

How a Book is Made

You will find many letters in this book.

This first letter is to YOU! It's from me. My name is Kath Donovan and I'm the person you can see on page 5. I'm a publisher.

This book tells you about itself. It shows you how it was made from start to finish.

I hope you enjoy this book.

Yours sincerely

Kath Donovan

Kath Donovan
Publisher

Heinemann Educational
A Division of Reed Educational
& Professional Publishing Limited

Registered Office
25 Victoria Street,
London SW1H 0EX

Registered in England 3099304
A member of the Reed [...]

What do I do first?

Look at the back cover of this book and see if you can find the word *Heinemann*. That's the company I work for.

I want someone to write a book about how we make books.

First I have to plan the book and choose an **author.**

Who writes the book?

As soon as I have chosen an author I send a letter like this. Today I am writing to Ms Lynch. I don't know her very well so I send her a **formal** letter.

> Here is the address I am sending the letter to.

> This is the name of the author I have chosen. Because it's a formal letter I use her title and her surname.

30 January 1998

Ms Emma Lynch
4 Duke Street
Rosemount Estate
LEEDS
LS23 1PZ

Heinemann

Halley Court
Jordan Hill
Oxford OX2 8EJ UK

Telephone +44 (0)1865 311366
Fax +44 (0)1865 314140
URL http://www.heinemann.co.uk
e-mail reed.educational@bhein.rel.co.uk
Direct Line

Dear Ms Lynch

How a Book is Made

I am currently publishing a new series of non-fiction books for Heinemann Publishers, and I am writing to ask if you would like to be one of the authors.

The book will be for 7–8 year olds and will explain how a book is made. As you have a great deal of experience in this area, I hope you will think about my suggestion.

I look forward to hearing from you.

Yours sincerely

Kath Donovan

Kath Donovan
Publisher

> The letter ends with my name and my job.

Heinemann Ed.

Emma Lynch is very pleased to get my letter. She writes back to me at once. Look at the dates on our letters.

Ms Lynch sends a formal letter back to me. She has put my name and address where I put hers in my letter. She has ended her letter in the same way as I did.

Emma Lynch
4 DUKE STREET ROSEMOUNT ESTATE LEEDS LS23 1PZ

1 February 1998

Ms Kath Donovan
Heinemann Publishers
Halley Court
Jordan Hill
OXFORD
OX2 8EJ

Dear Ms Donovan

How a Book is Made

Thank you for your letter of 30 January. I am very interested in the idea and I would like to write the book.

Perhaps we could use the making of *this* book to explain the publishing **process**. How about including some of the letters we write? I think this would help children to understand the part that letters play in the whole process.

I am in Oxford next week. Why don't we meet then to discuss the book?

I look forward to meeting you.

Yours sincerely

Emma Lynch.

Emma Lynch

Who plans the book?

I meet Emma Lynch. She agrees to write the book. Next, I introduce her to some of the people who will work with her. Then I give her a contract and a schedule.

HEINEMANN PUBLISHERS

This agreement is made on 10 February 1998

between

1. Heinemann Publishers of Halley Court, Jordan Hill, Oxford, OX2 8EJ, a division of Reed Educational & Professional Publishing Limited ('the Publisher')

and

2. Emma Lynch of 4 Duke Street, Rosemount Estate, Leeds, LS23 1PZ ('the Author')

DEFINITIONS

In this agreement:

1. 'The work' shall mean the book provisionally known as *How a Book is Made* for the Publisher's Literacy World non-fiction series.

2. 'Delivery date' shall mean the final manuscript delivery date set out in the schedule or another date agreed in writing by the Publisher.

3. 'Schedule' sha[...]
of this agreem[...]

A contract is a promise in writing. I promise to pay Emma if she agrees to write the book

I want the book ready by September. So I write a schedule. This is a list of all the jobs to be done.

How a Book is Made

Author: Emma Lynch **ISBN:** 0 435 09653 2
Stage: 1 **Extent:** 24pp

	Plan	Revised	Actual
Handover to designer	12/03/98		
First proofs to Heinemann	01/04/98		
First proofs to author / adviser	01/04/98		
Comments on first proofs back to designer	09/04/98		
Second proofs to Heinemann	20/04/98		
Comments on second proofs back to designer	27/04/98		
Third proofs to Heinemann	05/05/98		
Comments on third proofs back to designer	08/05/98		
Colour proofs to Heinemann	22/05/98		
Film to Heinemann	29/05/98		
Film to printer	03/06/98		

How will I make this book?

First I plan the book

I find an author
- I tell the author what I want in the book.
- The author agrees to write it.

The author writes a first draft
- The author sends it to me.
- I change some parts and send it back.
- This can happen a few times.
- The author sends the final draft to me.
- The editor checks it.

Next we send the book to the designer
- The designer plans how the book will look.
- A picture researcher chooses pictures or has photos taken.

Then we check the proofs
- Proofs are the first copies of the book.
- Many people check the proofs. We do it several times.
- When we are sure there are no more mistakes, we send the proofs to the printers.
- We choose the best cover.

Thousands of copies are printed
- Teachers buy the books.
- And, at last, YOU read them!

What is a manuscript?

Now Emma writes a **manuscript.** Then she sends me her **first draft.** I read the manuscript and then I send it to Gill. She's an adviser. I put a note to Gill in with the manuscript.

I know Gill well so I send her a note on a compliment slip. It's used for short, **informal** notes.

Heinemann

With Compliments

Gill,
Here's the 'How a Book is Made' manuscript. I've had a quick look at it and it seems fine. I'll give you a ring next week when we've both had a chance to read it properly.
Best wishes,
Kath

Heinemann Educational Publishers
Halley Court
Jordan Hill
Oxford OX2 8EJ
UK

Telephone +44 (0)1865 311366
Telex 837292 HEBOXF G
Fax +44 (0)1865 310043

R A member of the Reed Elsevier plc group

Page 4

<Heading> **How is a book made?**

Mock-up 1: *Letter from Kath to reader*

<Heinemann headed paper>

31 August 1998

Dear Reader

How a Book is Made

You will find many letters in this book.

The first letter is to YOU! It's from me. My name is Kath Donovan and I'm the person you can see on page 5. I'm a publisher.

This book tells you about itself. It shows you how it was made from start to finish.

We make some changes

I read the manuscript. So does Gill. We like it but there are some parts we want to change. So I write to Emma.

Heinemann

2 March 1998

Halley Court

Ms Emma Lynch
4 Duke Street
Rosemount Estate
LEEDS
LS23 1PZ

> I know Emma well by now, so this time I send her an **informal** letter. I use her first name and the letter is very friendly. When you have read it, look at the letter on page 6 again.

Dear Emma

How a Book is Made

I hope you're well and that you enjoyed the karate course. What a great way to forget about work!

I have read your manuscript and I have also had comments on it from an adviser. It's good news – we really like the manuscript. It is well written and the ideas flow well. You will need to make a few changes, though. I think some of the words you use are too difficult and in some places there are too many words on the page.

I've made a list of things you need to look at and have sent it with this letter. Please will you make these changes to your manuscript? Can you do this by next week?

Thank you for all the work you're doing. It's going to be a great book!

Best wishes.

Yours sincerely

Kath

Kath Donovan
Publisher

Heinemann Educational
A Division of Reed Educational
& Professional Publishing Limited

Registered Office
25 Victoria Street,
London SW1H 0EX

Registered in England 3099304

A member of the Reed Elsevier plc group

Emma looks at the parts we want to change. She changes the manuscript and sends us the **final draft.**

What is an editor?

Next I give the manuscript to Julie. She is the editor. Her job is to correct any mistakes before she sends it to the designer.

On this page you can see the marks that Julie puts on the manuscript. Look at page 23 to find out what they mean.

Page 15

Chooosing the photos

The photographer takes many photos. sally chooses the best ones for each page of the book. When they are ready they are sent to the design studio so that they ca

Page 16

Checking the proofs

Proofs have to be carefully c on the book to make sure tha and work well together. They times. There are first, second white. Finally there are colour book is printed. The proofing months.

<Caption>

First proofs usually have some mistakes in them. Corr marked on the proofs using signs like the ones that w manuscript (see appendix on page 23).

M E M O

To:	Jon Hicks	Re:	How a Book is Made
From:	Julie McCulloch	Date:	12 March 1998

Jon

This is one you'll like – it's a book about making a book! Let's hope it all runs smoothly (as if!).

Here is the manuscript on computer disk and on paper, together with a list of photos. The photos will be ready at the end of this week, so I'll pass them on then.

Let me know if you have any questions about the manuscript. I'm looking forward to seeing **proofs** on 1 April.

Thanks. *Julie*

Julie sends a memo to Jon, the designer. A memo is a note to someone in the same company. She knows Jon well so she uses his first name.

What will the book look like?

Jon plans how the words and pictures will fit together on the pages. When he has finished his plan he sends it to a design studio. Here they make the book into **proofs**.

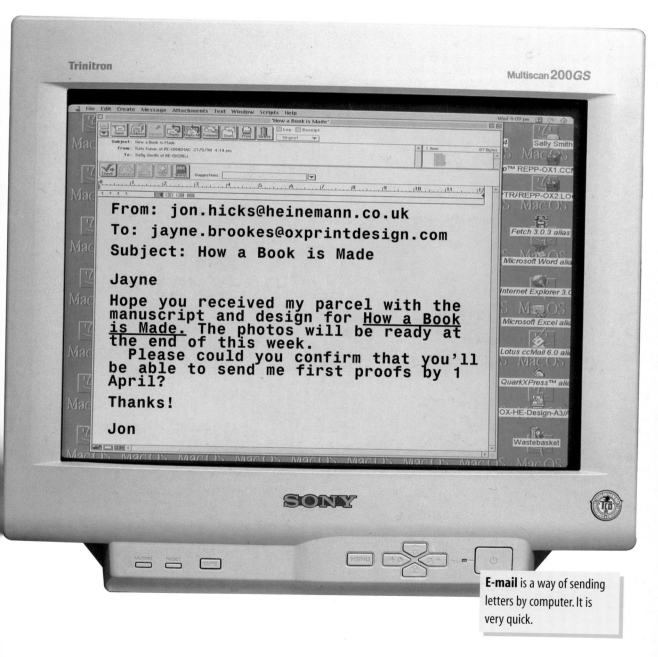

From: jon.hicks@heinemann.co.uk
To: jayne.brookes@oxprintdesign.com
Subject: How a Book is Made

Jayne

Hope you received my parcel with the manuscript and design for <u>How a Book is Made.</u> The photos will be ready at the end of this week.

   Please could you confirm that you'll be able to send me first proofs by 1 April?

Thanks!

Jon

E-mail is a way of sending letters by computer. It is very quick.

Who takes the photos?

Sally is the picture researcher. Her job is to think about pictures for the book. For this book she pays a photographer to take lots of photos.

Sally plans each photo. She tells the photographer what she needs.

Choosing the photos

Sally chooses the best photos for the book. Then she sends them to the design studio. There they fit the photos into the proofs.

Who checks the proofs?

When we get the proofs back we all check them very carefully. The pictures and the words must make sense. There must not be any mistakes.

The first, second and third proofs are black and white. The last set of proofs is in colour. Checking the proofs can take many weeks.

We correct the proofs just as we corrected the manuscript. We use the same sorts of marks.

Problems!

Things can go wrong! Julie, the editor, is worried because Emma has not sent the first proofs back. So she sends Emma a **fax.**

14 April 1998

Ms Emma Lynch
4 Duke Street
Rosemount Estate
LEEDS
LS23 1PZ

Halley Court
Jordan Hill
Oxford OX2 8EJ UK

Telephone +44 (0)1865 311366
Fax +44 (0)1865 314140
URL http://www.heinemann.co.uk
e-mail reed.educational@bhein.rel.co.uk
Direct Line

Fax: 0113 233 1898

Dear Emma

How a Book is Made

I've been trying to talk to you for a week now because I'm worried about the book.

You said you would send me your first proofs back, with captions for the photos, a week ago. The book is now running late and we might not be able to publish it in September, which will let a lot of people down.

Please ring me and let me know what is happening. I hope everything is OK.

Yours sincerely

Julie

Julie McCulloch
Editor

Julie writes an informal letter to Emma and sends it to her by fax. A fax is much quicker than the post.

Panasonic

Emma rings Julie as soon as she gets the fax. She forgot to post the proofs before she went on holiday!

Who chooses the cover?

The cover must look good and be clear to read. It must also show what the book is about. We hold a meeting to choose the best cover. Which one did we choose for this book?

Notes from the meeting – we send them to all the people who were there.

MINUTES OF COVERS MEETING

To: Kath D.
Julie M.
Jon H.
Sally S.

From: Rod S.

Date: 15 April 1998

How a Book is Made

- Cover A does not tell us what the book is about.
- Cover B is not very easy to read.
- Cover C is the best. It looks good. Use this one!

Testing

We often try out our books in schools before they are finished. The schools check for any problems before the book is printed.

Who prints the book?

The printer prints thousands of copies of the book. At the same time, our sales team visit schools to tell the teachers about the new book.

The books are kept in a big warehouse.

Published at last!

All I have to do now is wait for people to order the book. Because I am very pleased with this book I write to Emma to say thank you.

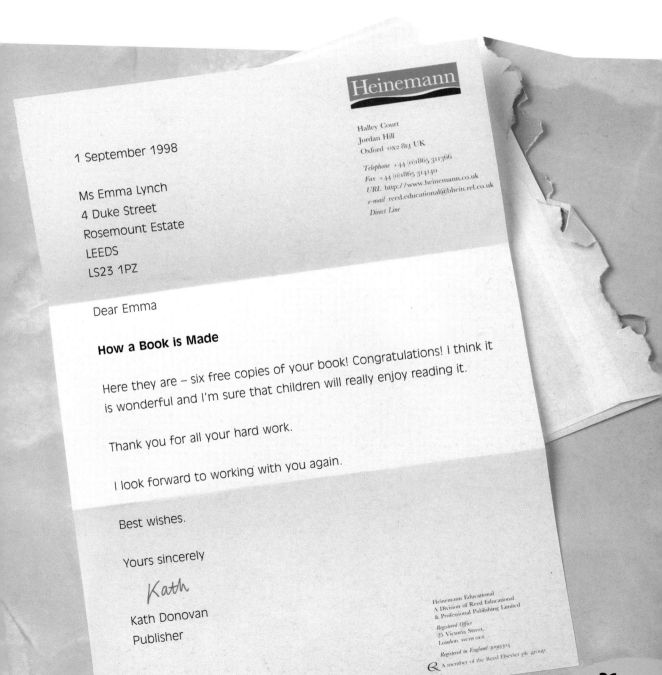

1 September 1998

Ms Emma Lynch
4 Duke Street
Rosemount Estate
LEEDS
LS23 1PZ

Heinemann

Halley Court
Jordan Hill
Oxford OX2 8EJ UK

Telephone +44 (0)1865 311366
Fax +44 (0)1865 314140
URL http://www.heinemann.co.uk
e-mail reed.educational@bhein.rel.co.uk
Direct Line

Dear Emma

How a Book is Made

Here they are – six free copies of your book! Congratulations! I think it is wonderful and I'm sure that children will really enjoy reading it.

Thank you for all your hard work.

I look forward to working with you again.

Best wishes.

Yours sincerely

Kath

Kath Donovan
Publisher

Heinemann Educational
A Division of Reed Educational
& Professional Publishing Limited

Registered Office
25 Victoria Street,
London SW1H 0EX

Registered in England 3099304

A member of the Reed Elsevier plc group

Who reads the book?

I was right! Lots of children and their teachers really like the book. Some of them write a letter to the author.

Langley Primary School
New Road
Langley
Buckinghamshire
MK19 4EP

9 October 1998

Ms Emma Lynch
4 Duke Street
Rosemount Estate
LEEDS
LS23 1PZ

Dear Ms Lynch

How a Book is Made

We have just read *How a Book is Made* and we really enjoyed it. We found out how books are made and how many people help to make them.

We liked all the different kinds of letters. Our favourite part was when the photographer took a horrible photo of Kath and it was in the book!

Yours sincerely
Rebecca David Ingrid
Mukesh Emma Natasha
Danny Paul Shamina
Monica
Class 3A
Langley Primary School

Glossary

author	a person who writes books
caption	a few words to explain a picture
e-mail	a message sent from one computer screen to another. It goes down a phone line.
fax	a message sent down a phone line from one fax machine to another. It prints out on paper.
formal	you write a formal letter to people you do not know well, or who are important
final draft	the version of the book that is printed after the author has made all the changes to it
first draft	the first version of a book that the author writes
informal	you send an informal letter to someone you know well
manuscript	the words written by an author
proofs	pages which show how the book will look. They are checked for mistakes before the book is printed.

Appendix – extra information

These are some of the special marks that are put on manuscripts and proofs to show changes that need to be made. They are a bit like a code.

take out a letter or letters

put in a letter or word

swop these words around

close this gap

join up

make this word **bold**

capital letter here

put a space in here

take out a letter and close up the gap

put in a hyphen (short dash)

23

Index